THE
MOMENTS
of
TRUTH

*A Book of Quotes and Short Stories to Enhance Life
by Building and Gaining Knowledge, Enlightenment,
Motivation, Reflection, and Perspective*

CALVIN S. JACKSON

Halo
PUBLISHING
INTERNATIONAL

Halo Publishing International
8000 W Interstate 10, #600
San Antonio, Texas 78230

First Edition, October 2022
Printed in the United States of America
ISBN: 978-1-63765-298-5
Library of Congress Control Number: 2022915776

Halo Publishing International is a self-publishing company that publishes adult fiction and non-fiction, children's literature, self-help, spiritual, and faith-based books. We continually strive to help authors reach their publishing goals and provide many different services that help them do so. We do not publish books that are deemed to be politically, religiously, or socially disrespectful, or books that are sexually provocative, including erotica. Halo reserves the right to refuse publication of any manuscript if it is deemed not to be in line with our principles. Do you have a book idea you would like us to consider publishing? Please visit www.halopublishing.com for more information.

First, giving honor to God for all His love, grace, and mercy. Without God, I am nothing! And I would be lost, dazed, and confused with no direction in my life. Thank you, God, for all the lessons and blessings throughout my life that helped me get to this point. Experiences are the best teachers, and all my test will continue to be testimonies of Your divine greatness. God is great no matter what!

Next, I must thank all my mom, my siblings, and all of my family. Thanks for your prayers, love and support, especially to my two beautiful children, Lorenz and Ciarah. Thank you both for saving my life and for always motivating me to establish a legacy for us and our family.

Lastly, I want to thank my Playa Made Brothers for always believing in me throughout my whole life. Also, I want to thank my coworkers in my recreational therapy department. Years ago, they started a list of my quotes and the phrases I say at work during the day with them or during processing with our clients at work. They called them: "Calvinism's." That was the seed that started this book, and I didn't even know it back then. But I do know God works in mysterious ways and I am so thankful and grateful for that.

Contents

Preface

One of the truest quotes of all time is, "If doesn't kill you, it will make you stronger." So, if you have been through major pain or have seen hardships in your life, remember life goes on, and life is a blessing no matter what because God is great no matter what! The moral of the story is: Death is the only thing final! Adversity, pain, & hardships makes you a stronger and better person. You also never know what another person is going through. Therefore, as a people we must share positive insight, testimonies, knowledge, experiences, and energy to help others keep going and never quit on life. It's easier said than done, but we must focus on the good things in life, not the bad--the love not the hate; the purposes not the pain; the future not the past. That's how you learn to move on and to move forward.

So, in reflecting upon these thoughts, I started to think of ways I could do my part. Also, remember as you get older, you get wiser too. And I started to think about times in my life when I could have made better decisions during crucial moments in my life. My "Moments of Truth" are what I like to call them. These are the truths that could really stay with me mentally during critical times so that I could make a positive decision to insure I had the best possible outcome for myself.

One day, I was feeling sad and depressed due to the divorce of my marriage. I was on my phone, scowling my social media platforms to kill sometime, and came across a post about Black History Leaders and some of their quotes for Black History Month. These were the real difference makers, the true legends who were born before their time: Martin Luther King, Jr. Malcolm X, Marcus Garvey, Harriet Tubman, Rosa Parks, etc.

Reading their words, I became focused, inspired and motivated again. It was the first time I had felt positive in months.

After that, I started writing and reading quotes to help me through my day as a way of positively coping, and as a positive distraction for my mind from all my stress. There were all kinds of quotes about God, overcoming, strength, love, pain, family, teamwork, hope, faith, and self-awareness. Then my passion for quotes started to make sense, especially noting that I have always loved quotes. In the past the quotes I sought out were related to playing sports, or to great coaches. And I have always loved historical people as well. And I've used quotes all the time processing groups with my military service members and kids at my job. Quotes have helped me in so many ways on so many levels. Quotes are dope! They are short, cool, smart, reliable, and easy to remember. They're something you can tell someone else, and with some real perspective and insight.

When I wrote quotes, it was a release. When I read quotes, it made me think. It was my new coping skill. Who doesn't want peace and knowledge in their life? It was a win-win situation for me. And everybody who knows me, will tell you I love to win! I loved it so much. And I want to help people in similar up and down life situations, so they won't have to go through things alone. Maybe I can help them prevent making the same dumb mistakes I did. You could say this is my way of paying it forward.

Writing a book was the easy part. Practicing what you preach and doing the things you write about was the hard part.

- Alex Pattakos, PhD. - Prisoner of our Thoughts

What are Moments of Truth?

Moments of Truth happen every day in our lives and they are always around us in the time spent with the family, in conversation with others, in interactions with co-workers, life experiences, etc. In our everyday life, we come across crucial times that matter most. These are the times that are connected to your memory, other people's memories, and decision making that affected your outcome forever, good or bad! That's why it's important to have more good life moments than bad ones. There are monumental moments where you had one chance to get it right and times in your past that you made a bad decision or spoke terrible comments. Those moments we can't get back. They were moments of immaturity, impulsiveness, and intrusiveness. Haven't we all said, "Woulda, Coulda, Shoulda" before? Those are the Moments of Truth. And I must say, I was too inconsistent during my moments. Therefore, I learned, we must be ready for them.

Everybody has ups & downs in life. And these life quotes will give you perspective and clarity before and during your Moments of Truth. Because in life, you only get one chance to make a good first impression. Life is too short to worry about the past and trying to fix mistakes.

This book contains quotes about God, hope, faith, love, pain, knowledge, strength, family, heart break, overcoming, pride, and self-worth from myself and other great, and random people as well. I'm going to offer my insight about the quotes and also how they helped me so much. Hopefully, I will touch on some things that people will relate to and benefit from. Enjoy. Thanks. God bless.

Part 1

God Is Love: His Grace & Mercy is Forever

1. **Faith without works is dead. - Unknown**

   We must show God we are all in for Him, like He is for us! So it important to have faith during good & bad times.

2. **Only God can judge Me. - 2Pac**

   Life is full of ups and downs. You might have to do something you didn't want to do to survive. People can't always understand your point of view, only God can. His option is the only one that matters anyway.

3. **God will break your heart to save your soul. - Unknown**

   This one touched me! As I encounter my own heart break, God uses it to make me a better person on all levels even during the most difficult times of my life. And it's worth it in the end, because heart breaks are temporary, but your soul lasts forever.

4. **Don't just pray to God when you need something. - Unknown**

   We can't be inconsistent with God if we want Him to be consistent with us.

5. **I love Jordan, Ali, Ruth, Gretzky, and Brady, but Jesus is the real G.O.A.T. (Greatest Of All Time) - Calvin Jackson**

   Nothing is greater that God and the Son of God. There is no greater sacrifice than what Jesus did for us and our souls.

6. **God is a Genius. He never makes mistakes.
    - Calvin Jackson**

    God is perfect in ever since of the word. We will never be perfect, but God wants us to believe in his perfect timing and his perfect Son, Jesus Christ.

7. **God is good. God is great. God is Love!
    - Unknown**

    And God's love will conquer all the hate in your life.

8. **Nothing will be impossible with God.
    - The Bible: Luke 1:37**

    Always believe that God has the final say so, not man.

9. **God will break you down to build you back up. - Unknown**

    A minor setback will always lead to a major comeback, if you work hard and keep the faith.

10. **If God is voting for you, some people are going to try tamper with the ballot to throw off your count. - Calvin Jackson**

    Some people will try to cheat you, rather than beat you. Cheaters never prosper in the game of life. Just don't make moves like them.

11. **If the Lord is for you, the world will be against you. - Unknown**

    God is the only One you need when you are in the biggest battles of life. But be aware and stay focused, because the enemy is everywhere.

12. **Don't stop & stare at what you don't have. That might blind you from what God has blessed you with. - Calvin Jackson**

   Always be grateful and thankful to God for what you have! Always!

13. **God has a purpose for you pain, a reason for your struggles, and a reward for your faithfulness. - Eric Thomas**

   Always have trust in God. His will, plans, and blessings are way better than you can imagine.

14. **God gave us two ears and one mouth for a reason. Listen more and talk less. - Calvin Jackson**

   Common sense ideas are not common, because people love to talk more than listen. But think about the ratio. It's better to be a great listener, than a great talker.

15. **God doesn't make things easier, he makes things possible. - Unknown**

   Life is hard, and things worth fighting for don't come easy. However, God is the best help you can find to get you through life.

16. **Man plans...God laughs. - Unknown**

   This is a true story by all means. Always make plans and set goals for yourself. But just know, life changes, people change, and nothing stays the same. So, set expectations only for yourself. At least this way, you and God can laugh together.

17. **God will turn your pressure into power. - TD Jakes**

    Just like pressure produces oil and diamonds, don't be scared. Just don't quit and trust God.

18. **The pain you are feeling can't compare to the joy that is coming. - The Bible: Romans 8:18**

    Hard times always hurt us, but God can change your situation for the better real quick. Have faith that He will and be willing to do the work. The reward will be richer than your sorrow.

19. **God doesn't give us things we can't handle. God helps us with the things we are given. - catholic.org**

    knows exactly what we need to make it through any situation in life.

20. **Marriage is really 50-50. That's why it is a must to involve God to just balance out the odds in your favor. - Calvin Jackson**

    Don't wait to ask God to help and bless your marriage. It might be too late, if you decide to wait.

21. **When God wants you to change and grow, He will make you uncomfortable. - Rev. Run**

    Growth can't happen while being comfortable, content, & complacent. We must be uncomfortable, disappointed, stressed, and challenged to grow in this lifetime.

22. **We pray for God to change our situation, but sometimes God puts us in those situations to change us. - Unknown**

    We only see half of the story. God sees all of it. He knows what's best and we must trust Him during difficult situations in life to make us better on all levels.

23. **The Lord works in mysterious ways. - Unknown**

    So don't ever question God! Just know, it will always work out in the end!

24. **Tears are prayers too. They travel to God when you can't speak. - The Bible: Psalms 56:8**

    Crying is weakness leaving the body, but God still knows its pain leaving your heart. Therefore, your tears are heard by God.

25. **Be careful on what you think, because your thoughts run your life. - The Bible: Proverbs 4: 23**

    You have to dream it before you achieve it. Thinking positive thoughts will help your mood, relationships, and goal setting. This is what manifestation in all about. God and the universe knows you personally, so please be kind to yourself. Produce positive thoughts and leave negativity out of your mind and heart.

26. **Don't mourn over voices that God has already muted. - Apostle Kevin Duhart, Sr.**

    You must stay positive and move forward without looking back to those who don't matter in your life anymore. God moves and replaces people for a reason.

27. **God will break you down & humble you to prepare you for your success. - Eric "ET" Thomas**

Success is a big deal. You must be ready for it if you want to keep it. But you must get ready for all the important things in your life.

28. **God responds to faith and prayer, not worry & doubt. - Calvin Jackson**

God wants us to know a brighter day is coming no matter how bad the storm is. You must believe with faith and never stop praying for your future.

29. **God will bless you, if He can trust you. - TD Jakes**

You must do your part to help God help you. Trust is key in any relationship. Show initiative and be consistent.

30. **It is impossible to please God without Faith. - The Bible: Hebrews 11:6**

We must do our part to show God our faithfulness and love. We must believe in a better day & never quit in life.

God is Everywhere &
God is Everything!

Ever since I was a little boy, I've known and felt God was always with me from positive people, vibes, energy, love, and with being safe in unsafe situations. Maybe, it was because my family was always in church when I was growing up. My mother, Connie, was the church pianist and my father, Frank, was a deacon at the church we went to. Both sides of my family have a strong connection to God. So, God has been in my life since day one. Ever since I could remember, God has been a positive force in my life, and I'm so thankful and grateful for that. I'm thankful for family that taught me about God, the Bible, morals, values, and the difference between religion and the spiritual being of God-that it's a part of the foundation to have the best relationship with Him.

If there is one thing I know, it is that to make it in life, you must have a solid relationship with God. Because there will be a time in our lives, from pain, heart break, illness, family issues, natural disasters, and any other unpredictable situations that life throws at us, where we will only have God to pray to and to rely on. This is why faith is so important. To trust God when you don't understand is a powerful mindset to have. We must know God is with us always and will never forsake us during any time in our lives. From every storm to every rainbow in your life, God is great no matter what!

The time, place, and moment I knew God was real and was with me was at my father's funeral. I will never forget it. It was a foggy, rainy morning in late October of 1997. It was the hardest day I ever had to face in my life.

Not only the worst day of my life, but I'd also torn my ACL at a basketball tournament a few weeks prior. Therefore, I had to walk on crutches at the dad's funeral and I couldn't play basketball to get away from all my stress, sadness and depression of losing my best friend.

During this type of storm, I was not myself. I started to question God, not care, not feel, and wanted to be rebellious. But this day taught me that God will never leave me or forsaken me. God will always bless the broken hearted during their time of pain or stress. Psalms 147:3 states: "He heals the brokenhearted and binds up their wounds." As a 17-year-old young man, I didn't really understand the grieving process yet. But I was going to get many lessons about grieve, love, strength, and God's grace and mercy firsthand.

As I mentioned earlier, my beautiful, smart, talented, awesome, loving mother, Connie Jackson, is a church pianist with an amazing voice. All my life, I was a accustomed to hearing my mom sing at church functions, weddings and funerals for other people all over the United States. It was a depressing couple of weeks for me, as I remember not talking nor eating much. So, I didn't know much about my father's home going celebration other than the date to mentally prepare for and what to wear to match my family. During the funeral my head was mostly down, and my eyes were full of tears.

As I sat next to my mom, I noticed her foot moving over to stand up out of the church pew. I could not believe it. My mom was approaching the pulpit to sing and show homage to my beloved father and her soulmate. It was the first time in weeks I was seeing light instead of darkness. It was so mind blowing to me that I could barely speak to think that my mom had enough strength to sing for my dad. As she started to sing one of his favorite songs, "My Soul Has Been Anchored in the Lord," I noticed the sun light shining through one of the church windows on her. The sky had been full of dark gray clouds and raining just 30 minutes before. It was a beautiful natural light with perfect timing. It was meaningful. It was symbolic. It was peaceful. It was divine. It was God!

After singing two of my dad's favorite gospel songs, I knew my mom was one of the strongest women in the world. Not because of weights & yoga, but because God's strength filled her mind, body, heart, and soul. It was a strong act because most people couldn't have done what she just did for our family.

Even to this day I still ask her, "Mom, How did you sing at dad's funeral?" And she always replies, "It was God's love, grace & mercy. When things are tough, I think of Jesus Christ, my Savior and His will. He went through so much more for us, so I get my strength from that."

I just nod and agree with her every word, because she is exactly right. She knows I love true stories with factual information, too. Because everything she says about God and Jesus is all facts! I think of my dad every day, because I miss him every day, and on my tough days,

I do remember what my mom told me about how she gets through her tough times. She is truly my angel on earth.

My father's death is still hard to talk about but, I love this story because on the toughest day of my life, I know God was with me and my family. That day made me look at life differently. It made me start a saying, "God is great No Matter What!" I still say that until this day. Like I mentioned before, I love true stories and factual information. And nothing is truer and more factual than God's will, plan, and promise for our lives, because God is everywhere and everything!

31. **Pray daily. Don't wish. God is real, not a genie. - Calvin Jackson**

    Praying is how you build a relationship with God; take it seriously. But know, most times God gives you what you need, over what you want.

32. **Grace is when God gives us good things we don't deserve. Mercy is when he spares us from the bad things we do deserve. Thank you, God, for your love, grace, and mercy. - Calvin Jackson**

    God is great no matter what and will always love us no matter what.

33. **The knowledge of God takes the fear out of you. - Minister Louis Farrakhan**

    Knowledge is power, and knowledge of God builds faith, character, confidence, strength, and integrity.

34. **When things are broken you can throw it away or let God put it back together and fix it. - Calvin Jackson**

    God can fix any problem in your life. Give it to Him and He will work on your behalf for the greater good.

35. **God will lift you up when, people let you down. - Calvin Jackson**

    People letting you down is going to happen in your life. God will never let you down like they did. Only expect things from yourself, not other people.

36. **The devil makes loud noises to distract you, but God makes beautiful silence to guide you. - Calvin Jackson**

    Where there is peace and silence, God is there. It makes total sense too. A moment of silence and prayer happens only when it's quiet.

37. **Faith is feeling the light with your heart, when your heart only seeing darkness in your life. - Calvin Jackson**

    You must know things will get better when you go through trials and tribulations. It can't rain forever, and we all know that rain bring rainbows.

38. **God will give you more when you let go. - Calvin Jackson**

    Worrying only brings stress & having doubt will create a negative mind state. God wants us to have peace.

39. **Rejection is God's way of saying, you are going in the wrong direction. - Unknown**

    God save us from ourselves all the time. Therefore, all rejection is not bad. Learn from it, so you will be prepared for next time.

40. **God doesn't make mistakes. - Unknown**

    God is perfect in every way possible! Just have faith in this word, and always trust in His plan for you and His will.

41. **You never realize God is all you need, until you realize God is all you have. - Unknown**

   God is always with you. And He will stay there with you especially when things change, and people change.

42. **Life is about knowing God, finding your purpose, and making a positive difference in someone else life. - Calvin Jackson**

   That's just a win, win, win, situation! I know it's easier said than done, but just keep working and having faith.

43. **God will always carry you through. - Max Lucado**

   Especially when you can't carry yourself anymore. Just don't give up on yourself when things get bad.

44. **Faith functions best when you don't know what's going to happen next. - TD Jakes**

   Don't assume. Just Believe! God is the only one that knows what is final in our lives, not man.

45. **When God tells you something, it might not always encourage you, but it will always inform you. - Calvin Jackson**

   God wants to help and save us. But sometimes that can't happen in a nice or happy-go-lucky way for us to really learn the lesson.

46. **God does not call the qualified. He qualifies the called! - Unknown**

    Don't let people hold you back. It's not up to them anyway! Nobody knows you like God, so let Him lead the way.

47. **Let us not love with words and speech, but with actions and in truth. - The Bible: John 3:18**

    Actions always speak louder than words.

48. **Don't hate yourself. You are made in the image of God. - Calvin Jackson**

    And there is no better image or better example than God. We are meant for great things.

49. **God will test you and bless you at the same time. - Nipsey Hussle**

    You might not understand the process at first, but you will understand why in the long run.

50. **God shall giveth and God shall taketh away. - Unknown**

    Don't take anything for granted. You never know how much time you got left. nothing last forever! I mean nothing!

51. **If God doesn't fix the situation, He's using the situation to fix you. - Unknown**

    Sometimes pain, betrayal and loss are the only ways we can learn valuable lessons to help us through life.

52. **Time is a luxury. To waste it on the wrong people and negativity is disrespectful towards God. - Unknown**

    God is too good and time is too priceless to spend it on the wrong people. Use your time wisely, because we can't get time back when it's gone.

53. **As someone thinks within himself, so he is. - The Bible: Proverbs 23:7**

    You are what you think you are. You are who you hang around with. You are what you do. You are how you feel about yourself.

54. **God plans are always more beautiful than your plans. - Calvin Jackson**

    Your plans, goals and dreams are cool. That's how you stay motivated in life. But you can't even image how great God's Plans are. That's why Drake made a song about.

55. **The devil will remind you of your mistakes of your past, God will remind you of your blessings in the present & future. - Calvin Jackson**

    Stop living in the past, it's unhealthy and can cause depression. You don't have a time machine and your future is brighter anyway.

56. **A real man always puts his wife and kids first. If he does that, God will put him first. - Minister Louis Farrakhan**

    All my real men out there… Take care of your family at all costs and by any means necessary. It is your responsibility and the reason you are on earth-to love, provide and protect!

57. **He who finds a wife finds a good thing and receives a precious gift from the Lord. - The Bible: Proverbs 18:22**

    It's simple, God is love, so you have to love your spouse like God loves the church.

58. **Never question who God removes from your life. He heard the negative conversation when you weren't around. - Unknown**

    God knows and sees all! Let Him help you or even save you by removing toxic people out of your life.

59. **Don't forget about God when you get what you prayed for. - Unknown**

    We must show God we are faithful during our lifetime, because He's faithful to us. Just consistent by praising Him during good and bad times.

60. **God helps those who helps themselves. - Benjamin Franklin**

    If you show initiative to help yourself, God and other people around you will show initiative to help us as well.

Passion & Purpose

For the last 17 years, I have had the privilege of working at Laurel Ridge Treatment Center, a mental health hospital in San Antonio, Texas. It is a 350-bed facility that services all types of people with all types of mental illnesses. I respect our hospital because we want to help everybody, from the 4-year-old baby in C.P.S. to the 80-year-old military veteran, and every age in between. We take people from every race, gender, religion, culture, and creed at our hospital. We do our best to educate and teach positive coping skills to all our clients while they are with us. So, when they leave us, our clients can live their best life possible while managing their mental health issues.

During my tenure at Laurel Ridge, I have been a Mental Health Worker (a tech on the floor with clients), CPR/CPI Trainer for new hires, Driver & Transporter in the Transportation department, Sports Coach for the UT Charter School on our campus, and an Activity Recreational Specialist in the Specialized Therapeutic Services Department. I've been blessed to win Employee of the Year, due to starting recreation programs for our military active-duty clients and our residential adolescent clients. I started a basketball team for coworkers to build teamwork and morale in the workplace as well. I love my job, my recreation therapy team, and our clients. And with almost two decades of working in this field, you can guarantee that I've seen and experienced many different things, good and bad. When you are working with people, dealing with people, and helping people anything can happen at any moment.

During my time in college and my tenure at Laurel Ridge, I coached youth sports: AAU Basketball, TYFA Football, Little League Baseball, softball, track, and I was a Cheer Dad once too. I love all sports, teaching, coaching, sportsmanship, competition, and helping people get better as a whole. Everything connected with sports is a big passion of mine. I've also always had the gift of gab. So, communication skills to help others became another passion of mine as time went on.

I'm truly blessed to get paid for coaching kids & helping people every day. I know I have the power to make a positive difference in someone else's life when they're having a difficult time. It's a responsibility I take seriously, and I give 110 percent effort because my words, actions, feedback, and attitude can make all the difference in the world for my kids and clients. I have many stories about my passions at work, but the best stories I have are when God shows me my purpose and that He's always with me.

Three years ago, I was going through a tough divorce and found myself dealing with depression and anxiety. This was foreign to me because I was the person helping people with depression and anxiety. But as a leader, professional, and provider, I had to face what faced me and do what I had to do to move forward in the best way I could, while maintaining a strong work ethic. But one morning, I woke up defeated, sad, and confused. It's that pain that hurts your heart so much that you wish you were numb and didn't feel anything at all. I did not want to go to work because I didn't want to be around anyone. But

I couldn't call in because I had a young children's group at 9am by myself. So, I prayed for strength and focus and went to work like a normal day like I usually do.

One thing about all the kids' units is that they love recreational therapy. To them, recreational therapy is the fun group of the day. They expect it to be an awesome activity because of our high standards in my department. Therefore, I show the most initiative and effort with our kids and adolescents' units, because they deserve the best and the best me possible. On our kids' units, we admit Child Protected Services children at times to help the south region of Texas by letting kids stay with us to get treatment before they go to their new home or new placement situation.

One of our C.P.S. clients, named Johnny, was one of the children who had stay with us for over 30 days while he waited for his adoptive family paperwork to get approved by the state. Johnny was an awesome 5-year-old with ADHD and disruptive behavior disorder. Which means he was a very hyper child with minimal focusing ability and poor impulse control. Every day on and off the unit, Johnny needed redirection and help from staff to stay on task due to his negative behaviors. Let just say Johnny was really cute, but also really bad at times. But of course, all of our staff loved him anyway.

The morning was down and out, I did an exercise group in the backyard of the unit with the kids. We played Capture the Flag and relay races for the group, so the kids could run out some energy and process the importance of teamwork and endorphins. I should have known God was with me then, because He knows how I love the kids and that was my first group of the day. He knows how kids keep me smiling and feeling young because of their positive energy, too.

But after group, I was still sad because of my reality and wanted to be alone to think and write notes about the group in peace and quiet. So, I stayed in the backyard as all the kids went inside the unit for their next therapeutic group. While sitting outside and writing notes, I started to cry and felt alone. A couple of minutes went by, Johnny came running out the unit back outside to get his shoes that he had thrown earlier at one of his peers during my group. As the most hyper kid ever, he walked calmly towards me to get his shoes and asked, "What's wrong, Mr. Calvin? Are you crying?" I replied, "No Johnny, I'm good Lil Homie. It's my allergies." Then he said, "I get allergies sometimes too when I cry." As I started to smile, Johnny looked me in the eye and told me, "Don't be sad, Mr. Calvin. We love you. It's going to be okay." I replied, "I love all y'all too, Johnny." I then gave him a high-five before I let him back into the building.

Then suddenly, it was like the old Johnny returned because after entering the building he threw his shoes again at one of his peers. That was hilarious by the way. But I was so shocked and flabbergasted that this baby in Child Protected Services with no parents cared enough about me to ask what was wrong, and tell me it's going to be okay, and that he loved me. Wow! Unbelievable! I just looked up at the sky and said, "Thank You, Lord." I knew God was with me and I wasn't alone. I knew God used Johnny as a vessel to connect with me to help me remember my passion, plans, goals, and purpose.

That's what makes God so great. He can use anybody or anything to bless your life. It was so amazing to me that a child could make more sense to me than my friends and family members who had told me the same thing. That day made me refocus and re-establish my mindset to help me realize that God is great no matter what you go through in life! Because God's plan and will is so much better than our plans. So, why worry? It made me realize, I must try to be the very best I can be for God, myself, my family, my legacy, and all the people that depend on me and love me.

Always focus on your passions and purpose in life, because at the end of the day that's what is going to keep you happy, focused and blessed. You can be a blessing for someone else, just like Johnny was a blessing to me, and hopefully, just as I was for him.

61. Praising God in the sunshine is easy. But praising Him in the darkness is the hard part. - Calvin Jackson

Good and bad things happen to the just and unjust alike. Therefore, God is always worthy to be praised no matter the situation.

62. If you can't change it, and God has allowed it, you need to find a way to prosper in it. - Dr. Tony Evans

You can't change or control everything, but you must try to find the bright side to everything.

63. No matter how, where, or when, all men will kneel before God. - Calvin Jackson

Not only out of respect for God should we kneel. There will be a time your heart will be so broken you won't be able to stand when you pray.

64. Let God transform you into a new person by changing the way you think. - The Bible: Roman 12:2

God will always make you better and help you evolve to the next level if you think about your goals, dreams, and blessings.

65. When you can't see clearly, God will send you a sign in plain sight. So, pay attention! - Calvin Jackson

Signs, patterns, and gut feelings are warnings from our guardian angels.

66. God will make a way out of no way! - Unknown

Read the stories of Moses, David, Joshua, and Daniel! God can and will guide you through anything. Just don't quit and trust the process.

67. God will always use your struggle and pain for your good. - Calvin Jackson

It may not be quick and easy, but it's for a reason and only for a season. Keep fighting for a better day. Your burden or situation is going to help and bless somebody else.

68. God is good, all the time and all the time, God is good. - Unknown

This is a classic quote because two people usually say this together to agree that God is a positive force in their life.

69. God makes this promise: You ask, and you shall receive. And God always keeps his promises. - Unknown

You must speak positive things into existence. You must let God know your plans, so He can help you accomplish your goals.

70. When God gives you a new beginning don't make the old mistakes. - Unknown

God will not continue to give you chance after chance to get something right. Learn from your mistakes and correct your wrongs.

71. **For whenever our heart condemns us, God is greater than our heart, and He knows everything. - The Bible: 1 John 3:20**

Give your heart to God and He will help you get through any heart break and disappointment.

72. **God will put you back together right in front of the people that broke you. - Ice Cube**

God will make all things righteous, so don't worry about your enemies. Therefore, don't waste time plotting and scheming for revenge. Success is the best revenge anyway!

73. **Only God can turn a mess into a message. A test into a testimony. A trial into a triumph. A victim onto a victory. - Unknown**

It's not how you start; it's how you finish. Don't worry about the past, because the present and the future has so much more in store for you.

74. **Trust God will put the right people in your life at the right time and for the right reasons. - Unknown**

Don't force relationships. Don't force love. Don't chase people. Let things and people flow naturally to your life.

75. **The devil loves to take something beautiful and ruin it. God loves to take what's ruined and make it beautiful. - @ GetThroughTheWeek**

Don't let the devil destroy you, let God design you.

76. **God will take you through troubled water, because your enemies can't swim. - Calvin Jackson**

    Don't worry about enemies, haters, negative people, and naysayers. Just keep swimming like Dory.

77. **Trouble don't last always, because God's love always last. - Calvin Jackson**

    God's plan and will are perfect, so He knows the best time and the exact time to help us and bless us.

78. **Lord my God, You have done many miracles. Your plans for us are many. If I tried to tell them all, there would be too many to count. - The Bible: Psalm 40:5**

    God has been taking care of us before birth. He has done so many great things for us, we don't even remember them all. And He will continue to take care and bless us if we have faith in Him.

79. **GOD doesn't deal with problems; He deals with promises. - Jeremy Foster**

    God looks at problems and difficult issues differently than us. We see the burden within heartbreak, He sees the lesson within the blessing.

80. **God didn't bring you this far to leave you. Your greatest days are still in front of you. - Joel Steen**

    If you are here still alive, fighting the good fight for the Lord, you're blessed. He will never forsake you. Keep moving forward with prayer and faith.

81. **God has already worked it out. Stop worrying and stressing over it. - Bishop Don Magic Juan**

    Always have faith in the Lord and don't overthink stuff that you can't change. Overthinking, stress, and worry only takes away from your joy and happiness.

82. **God is a gentleman. He will open all your doors. - InstaGOD**

    He will show compassion, bring you gifts, show you love and express kind words to you as well. He's always great to be around, too. God is the gentleman of all gentlemen.

83. **For God has not given us a spirit of fear and timidity, but of power, love, and self-discipline. - The Bible: 2 Timothy 1:7**

    Show your true self, which the Lord has made you to show. Fear is the complete opposite of faith. And power, love, and self-discipline are major keys towards self- mastery.

84. **You don't have to be approved by man, if you are appointed by God. - Godquoted**

    Opinions from others don't matter. God knows your name, mind, heart and soul. Only God can judge me! In my 2Pac voice.

85. **Have glory in your suffering, because we know that suffering produces perseverance, character, and hope. - The Bible: Roman 5:3**

    Always turn your pain into purpose. Use it as fuel to motivate you and conquer all your goals and dreams in life.

86. **You are God's masterpiece. - The Bible: Ephesians 2:10**

    Therefore, you must carry yourself like a one-billion-dollar piece of art. And let's be honest; there is no better painter, designer, and creator than God.

87. **Don't worry what people say behind your back, because God is going to bless you in front of their faces. - Unknown**

    Everybody will have some haters and naysayers cross your path. Just kill them with kindness and let God handle the rest.

88. **Forgive the people that hurt you. God will bless you with double the joy and double the victory. - Unknown**

    Holding grudges is unhealthy and brings a vast amount of negative energy. Always remember, forgiveness is for you to have peace, a healed heart, and a sound mind.

Family Ties

I'm a loyal, pride-filled, family-oriented Texan. From the westside of San Antonio, Texas to be exact. I lived off Culebra Rd.; my grandmother lived on Popular St. and my best friend, Javier, lived by Thomas Jefferson High School. My friends and I swam at Woodlawn Lake Pool during the summers and played basketball at the legendary Frank Garrett Center all year round.

I loved my whole neighborhood because I had family everywhere and it was full of love and pride. But, growing up in the 1990's on the westside, eastside, and southside of San Antonio was very tough at times. These areas had many projects/courts, a low number of resources, high crime rates, a vast number of gangs, drug dealers, and drug addicts. Trouble was easy to get into, but very hard to get out of. And if you need more proof, in the 1990's D.J. Quik made a hit rap song, "Just Like Compton" with a verse about a true story at his concert in San Antonio, Texas.

It was one of those cool, but very bad moments, for my city. Many God-fearing families lived in these tough areas and displayed strong faith during bad times. Families did their best in difficult situations and tough circumstances. For example, my cousins and I didn't know how poor we were until we got older. Even with bad things around us at times, we were raised by a village that taught us about God, love, faith, respect, morals, and values.

Just like every inner-city in America, parents put their kids in sports to have a positive outlet, develop coping skills, and for distraction. And let's be honest, youth sports help kids with teamwork, discipline, sportsmanship, and work ethic, which are great skills to have to help you through your whole life. When I was 13, I played AAU Basketball with the St. Ann Saints, a historic Catholic church on the westside of San Antonio. Sometimes we went to mass together as a team with our coach as a team building exercise. We were a solid team with a mix of solid players in our area. Some guys were my classmates; some guys were my rivals during the basketball seasons.

One of my teammates, Kelvin Franks, was like a play-cousin to me. We grew up together and our families went to the same church together, West Mt. Nebo Baptist Church. Our dads were deacons of the church, and our moms were in the choir together. And we clicked because our names were similar. Kelvin had an older brother, Kevon. He was four years older than us and went to Thomas Jefferson High School. Kevon was a great big brother and was cool with everybody who had love for him and his family. However, Kevon was one of the leaders of the neighborhood gang, The Lincoln Court Gangers , otherwise known as the L.C.G.'s. Kevon was loved by few, respected by many, and feared by all. The main reason, nobody messed with Kelvin and his friends, was because most people didn't want those problems nor become enemies with Kevon.

Speaking of problems, Kevon started getting into a lot of trouble from fights, skipping school, and even getting arrested at the Frank Garrett Multi-Purpose Center. Kelvin's parents were hurt and embarrassed for the last time. After bailing Kevon out, his parents made him go into the Army to get away from the gang life, to learn discipline, and to have a brand-new start for a better in life with a brighter future. Kelvin was able to write him, but he could not go to Washington D.C. to see Kevon where he was stationed.

A year went by, and Kevon finally came home to visit. We were so excited to see and talk to him. And all of us were in for a grand surprise. Kevon was a brand-new man. Not only was he a strong United States soldier, but he was also studying to become a Nation of Islam Muslim. I guess he wanted to be the best black man he could be for himself, his family and community. He started telling Kelvin & I about Allah (God), Malcolm X, Elijah Muhammad, Minister Louis Farrakhan, and some of the disciplines that came with being Muslim. Everybody was so happy Kevon was an educated man with morals now, and not a menace to society like he was in the past.

The morals of the story are, God is love, therefore God will be within you and your whole family. No matter the level of spirituality or level of religion. Also, if God can change and help young men like Kevon, He could change and help anybody. If God sees you showing effort and initiative, He will show effort and initiative with you. God is everywhere, in all things, forms and situations.

Growing up as you can see, I had information about the Baptist, Catholic, and Muslim faiths and religions. I honestly think if it's Jesus, Star of David, Buddha, Ra, Ja, or Allah, God just wants us to come to Him and have a relationship with Him. No matter how you get there, He wants you to come and build something great with Him. God will receive you with open arms filled with love, grace, and mercy no matter the situation. God is a perfect genius that has plans better than you can ever imagine for yourself. Trust Him and put Him first in your life, and watch greatness happen in your life!

Calvin S. Jackson • 53

89. **Faith doesn't make sense. That's why it makes miracles. - John DiLemme**

   Having faith is hard sometimes, especially during a dark time in your life. But we should never stop believing in a brighter day and overcoming the impossible with God's love.

90. **God minus the world equals God. But the world minus God equals zero. - Laurence W. Wood**

   We are nothing without God, but we are everything with God.

91. **Start your prayers by saying, "Thank You." - Beth L. Olson**

   Prayer is not a wish list request. It is honest conversation with God from your heart. So, show thanks and gratitude towards God every chance you get.

92. **Luck is like an atheistic word for God. - Peter Thiel**

   Always remember, you are not lucky, you are blessed by the grace, mercy, love, and favor of God.

93. **God will turn your private prayer to public testimony. - Gods_Feed_Daliy**

   God plans to turn your losses into a victory. And winners tell the best stories of overcoming, that will help other people during their journey.

94. **Be still and know that I am God. - The Bible: Psalm 46:10**

When we are still, we can't be impulsive or rushed. Being still is also being at peace. We must always remember the power of God. He is the Alpha and Omega, so He delivers us from any negative situation in our lives.

95. **When your heart is pure and true, God has a way of making sure everything works out in your favor. - GODs_Feed_Daily**

Having a true and pure heart is a quality some people can't understand. Those are some qualities of Jesus, so you know God loves when we show that.

96. **God doesn't give us what we have the power to get for ourselves. - Devon Franklin**

If you show initiative for yourself, positive things are bound to start happening in your life.

97. **You can trust God and also see a therapist. - @theanchoredplace**

Trusting and talking to God is the easy part. Talking to a stranger, one on one, about your problems, depression, and anxiety is a very hard thing to do. But God wants us to take care of our mental health at any cost. So, finding someone you trust to talk to can be a blessing in your life.

98. **Beloved, let us love one another for love is of God. And everyone that loveth is born of God, and knoweth God. He that loveth not knoweth not God. For God is Love. - The Bible: 1 John 4:7-8**

   God is love, and if we are an image of Him, we must show and give love to others. We must be loving and caring even when we are in pain and depressed. Have faith and trust in the Lord no matter what happens.

99. **God will make greatness out of a great mess. - Unknown**

   In the Bible they're tales about how all the disciples had flaws and made mistakes, but God used them for the greater good anyway.

100. **I love God, because even though I deserve nothing, He gave me everything. - Unknown**

   God will always show us grace and mercy even when we don't deserve it.

101. **Don't wait until Sunday to thank God. Thank God every day. - Calvin Jackson**

   You have to give to get in life, and any real relationship is about give or take. Think about it, God just doesn't bless you on Sundays at church.

102. **Faith in God includes faith in His timing. - Unknown**

   Ups and downs, Trials and tribulations, Pain and heart break is inevitable. So just have faith and believe God will get you through the worst of times, perfectly on time.

103. Those who walk with God always reach their destination. - Spirit Identify

Life is a journey with many different uncontrollable situations. But what you can control is who with you on your journey of life. Family, friends, and support systems are wanted. But to make it, only God is needed.

104. But without faith, it is impossible to please God. - Hebrews 11:6

God wants you to give your problems to Him. To let go and let God is a part of life. Worrying upsets God, which gives the devil joy.

105. Things change. People change. Places change. Families change. Friends change. Careers change. Spouses change. Wealth changes. But God will never change. - Calvin Jackson

Many things will change on you and let you down in life. But God will never let you down, leave you, or quit on you, which will lead you to change for the better as life goes on.

106. God will cut the grass in your yard of life, to expose the snakes, bugs, flees, & ticks that you must avoid. - Calvin Jackson

You must pay attention, stay focused, and always be aware of your surroundings in life.

107. **Let your love for God change the world. But never let the world change your love for God. - Stacy L. Sanchez**

Don't let worldly things change you. You are stronger than social media, drugs, porn, and your enemies. Let God change you to be the best version of yourself.

108. **Stress comes from trying to do it all on our own. Peace and serenity come from putting it all in God's hands and letting go. - Unknown**

God doesn't mind taking on your stressful problems. He wants to help us evolve and grow by having a relationship with Him.

109. **If God brought you to it, He will bring you through it. - Strength In Verses**

God doesn't make mistakes. Your situation, pain, heartbreak, and disappointments are only for a season and for a reason. Just learn from it and move forward.

110. **Heart break and pain are real. That's why you have to be real when you pray to God, so your healing can be real. - Calvin Jackson**

God is the realist and the Truest! You must have faith and believe that your problems are nothing compared to the grace and mercy of God.

111. **When you get what you want that's God's direction. When you don't get what you want that's God's protection.**

   We should always want God's direction and protection. When God moves on your behalf, it will happen for you. And if it is meant to be, it will be. Just trust, have faith, and believe in the Most High.

112. **The giant in front of you is never bigger than the God inside of you. - Unknown**

   You heard of the epic story of David and Goliath, right? God can conquer and help you overcome any fear or evil in your life.

113. **When God delivers you from evil, don't keep in touch or reconnect with that situation. - Unknown.**

   Moving forward is a part of God's plan. Don't go back to old negative ways, bad habits, and toxic relationships.

114. **We have all given God a million reasons not to love us. None of them changed his mind. - Unknown**

   God is Love, and His love is forever, unconditional, timeless, everlasting, and eternal. He will never stop loving us, no matter what we do.

115. **People will hurt and humiliate you. Meanwhile, God is healing & magnifying you. - Calvin Jackson**

   People will change on you, quit on you or disappoint you. But God will always be there to lift you up after those let downs.

116. **God gives us things to share. God does not give us things to hold. - Mother Teresa**

   The only reason God blesses us, is so we can bless other people.

117. **You must give God some of your time. - Unknown**

   God is worth your time, especially when we ask Him for so much. There are no excuses when you got church, prayer, meditation, confession, volunteer work, etc.

118. **Mornings are so much better when you pray & talk to God first. - @JesusOfHope**

   When talk to God first, that means He's the first one on your mind. If you stay consistent with this routine of prayer, He will become first in your life.

Waiting On God

Have you ever felt insignificant or not good enough? How about been down and out with sadness, depression, and anxiety? Have you ever been stuck in toxic relationships, dead end jobs and around untrustworthy friends and family members? I know I have. These are the times we must show initiative for ourselves with great decision-making skills and take a step out on faith to better our situation. But during this time, we must wait on God's plan to bless us at the right time.

All great plans take time and God's plan and timing are always perfect. Therefore, no matter the season of your life, you must know and believe that. The hard part is being patient and waiting on God when you are trying to improve your life. That's why patience is a virtue, because it is hard as hell to master. And I want to be really honest and transparent with y'all. I have no patience whatsoever. I'm the guy mad at the traffic lights if they are taking too long to change. I'm a focused and business-minded person that has many things to do. Therefore, I feel I need to rush at times to stay on task to accomplish my goals. However, I'm working on my patience because I've learned that waiting is always a part of life. And for the most important things in your life, you're going to have to work hard for and it will always be worth the wait in the end. God also delays things to help protect you.

Waiting is so valuable because it's showing God and yourself that quitting is not an option. You're going to stay the course with faith in your heart and hope on your mind. I'm a member of Resurrection Baptist Church, and my pastor explained what to do when you're waiting on God.

One thing about Pastor Ray Brown is that he always makes it simple and plain with facts from the Bible so that everyone can understand and learn. That's why I love to hear him preach. This message helped me so much, I had to share my notes with y'all.

The first thing we must do while waiting on God is to always thank Him in advance for all the blessings that are about to come. During good times and bad times, thank God. During storms and sunshine, thank God. During smiles and frowns, thank God. Ups and downs are a part of life to help us understand life and appreciate life. Good and bad things happen to the just & unjust alike. Therefore, always thank God! This is a key component because it shows true faith and tells God that you trust His will and His plan for your life. Everybody's life is different, and nobody's life is perfect. So, you might as well show love, gratitude, a positive attitude, class, work ethic, and faith during the process of growth. Let God lead the way and guide you through the journey of life, so you can win before the end of your journey of life.

The second thing we must do while waiting on God is to build a strong relationship with Him. We must thank Him for all is love, grace, and mercy at all times. I pray daily, sometime multiple times a day, to show my respect and thanksgiving. Meditation, a moment of silence, going to church, reading the Bible and any characteristic of Jesus

Christ are all good too. It's important to remember every great relationship has a two-way street of give and take. We should know all the great things God has given us. Therefore, it only makes sense to try to give God back greatness in return. We must talk to God in our prayers. We must do our very best to also listen to God. God can appear to us how He wants and in many different ways, we must just pay attention and be ready. God will be a voice of reason, numbers, animals, a vivid dream, a strong gut feeling, a sign of any kind, and a consistent thought in your mind. Our job is to never give up or to quit on ourselves. We must trust God at all times and know His love will reign forever.

The third thing and last thing we must do while we are waiting on God, is to always serve God. Serve in any way you can, at any time you can. We must show compassion, love, kindness, hope, forgiveness, courage, and faith to ourselves and others, which are some the attributes of Jesus Christ. You can give back to the less fortunate, donate food and clothes, volunteer time for a positive cause, coaching kids, starting programs to help others, etc. God just wants to use us to bless others, help others, and show love to others in any way we can. Serving God will never be a waste of time, energy, money, or effort in your life either. However, we often let other things and people in our lives waste our time, energy, money and effort. Things and people change, but God never changes! You can serve God by giving your testimony after your test, too. We all have been though tough tests in life. So, it's very important that we share our stories, problems, and knowledge, to pay it forward to bless someone else. Always remember God loves us so much, He wants some of your time, and faith without works is dead. So, serve with dignity, discipline, and determination to please God, and to stay consistent on your journey of serving God.

In conclusion, be patient and know better days are coming. All your hard work and faithfulness will pay off eventually. You must know and believe that in your heart, mind, and soul. God is a genius and His timing, plan, and will are perfect. Just stay the course, stick to the plan, keep the faith, smile every day, love yourself, love others, and thank God during good and bad times. So, remember, thank God in advance, build a relationship with God, and serve God in anyway you can. These amazing steps help your outcomes and your evolution of life. This is how we use our time wisely, grow as people, and get better at the unpredictable situations during our journeys. It's our job to be ready for the opportunities that God will bless us with so that we can reach our full potential in achieving all our goals and dreams, which come from our passions and purpose in life.

119. **God is indeed my salvation; I am confident and unafraid. For the Lord is my strength and my might and He has been my salvation. The Bible: Isaiah 12:2**

God will deliver you from, evil, harm, ruin, loss, and sin. Why should you be afraid or fear anything?

120. **God is always closer to the broken hearted. - Trent Shelton**

God knows all about your heartbreak, tears, pain, trials and tribulations in life. He wants to help us all heal and overcome sorrow.

121. **God can give us joy without things, but things without God will never give us joy. - Unknown**

Joy that comes from love, family, friends, memories, and God last forever. Joy that comes from material things, like money, cars, and clothes doesn't last long.

122. **People look at the outward appearance, but God looks at the heart. - The Bible: 1 Samuel 16:7**

God doesn't care about looks, materials, money, or status. He cares about how you treat the people during your lifetime.

123. **God will do something to you on purpose so you can start having purpose. - Josh Shelby**

When you have a higher calling and a bigger purpose, God will stop your plans to make sure His come in fruition for the greater good.

124. **When God says "Action" in your movie of life, not a single person can say "Cut". - Calvin Jackson**

Let God direct your movie and all your moves. Don't let actors be the directors in your life story when you and God are writing the script.

125. **Don't confuse yourself with what God wanted you to go through, instead of what you decided to deal with. - Bishop Don Magic Juan**

Sometimes we hold ourselves back and don't even know it. But know, God will never waste his love and time on anything.

126. **Whatever God removes, He will always replace. - Unknown**

God shall giveth and taketh away. So, people, places, and material things will come and go. Just have faith God is going to give you better and back more than you asked for.

127. **God calls us to walk by faith, not talk by faith. Faith involves your mind, heart, and feet. - Dr. Tony Evans**

You just can't talk about having faith and talk about loving God, you must show it. Faith without work is dead. Don't talk about it, be about it.

128. **When you pray, God listens. When you listen, God talks. When you believe and have faith, God works. - Strength in Versus**

Simple directions and guidelines for your life. Use them and be consistent for the best results.

129. God will repay each person according to what they have done. - The Bible. Romans 2:6

Nobody is perfect! But God wants us to evolve as life goes on. We must love, pray, have faith, help others in need, be righteous, give Him time, read the Bible, and believe in His word.

130. Put on the whole armor of God, that you may be able to stand against the wiles of the devil. - The Bible: Ephesians 6:11

To fight the devil, you must have all your weapons to beat him, because he's going to come at you from different ways. With God you will win in the end. But you're going need your faith, prayers, chest plate, shield, sword, sling shot, rod, staff, the Bible to help you out.

131. Do not let your heart be troubled. Trust in God. Trust also in Me. - Jesus Christ

Trust is a hard thing to give in any relationship in life. But, lucky for you, God makes all relationships with Him loving, peaceful and joyful.

132. Things go wrong in your life, so God can manifest His glory in your life. - Pastor Ray Brown

God wants the best for you in all situations. So, pray, have faith, and believe His word. Grace and mercy from God will always give you glory.

133. God will do something on purpose to make you have purpose and walk towards your purpose. - Calvin Jackson

Everybody on this earth has a purpose in life. Sometimes it's hard to find that's why God has to help us, push us, and evolve us to make sure we know what it is.

134. Blessed are the peacemakers for they shall be called the children of God. - Unknown

Peacekeepers, will avoid conflict, turn a blind eye, and overlook things to keep the peace. Peacemakers will do whatever it takes to make peace from helping others, fighting battles, and being a leader in difficult situations.

135. Fear not, believe only. - Jesus, The Bible - Luke 8:50

In my opinion, these may be the four strongest words in this whole book from the only perfect person to ever walk the earth.

136. The will of God will never take you where the grace of God will not protect you. - Bernadette Devlin

God will never forsake you no matter how bad you feel or how bad it gets. God will also never give you anything you can't handle. Don't quit, believe and have faith and God will deliver.

137. God will lead you where He wants you to be, but you have to talk to Him daily to see where He wants you to go. - Unknown

Make sure you have a personal relationship with God. Just trust in His plan and His will. It is way better than your plans anyway. Prayer is key during your process.

138. God's way is perfect. All the Lord's promises prove true. He is a shield for all who look to Him for protection. - The Bible - Psalm 18:30

Perfect means having all the required or desirable elements, qualities, or characteristics that are as good as it is possible to be; to make something completely free from faults to defects. Absolute; Complete.

139. God is a master at turning unfair things into miracles when we let him. - Dr. Tony Evans

God loves when people with difficult life situations turn their pain into purpose. That's how goals and dreams are manifested.

140. No matter how strong you are, you will have to go to God for strength. - Calvin Jackson

In your weakest moments, God is the only one that will give you ultimate strength in all areas to overcome.

141. The Bible is the blueprint. God is the architect. You are the carpenter. - T.D. Jakes

My dad was a carpenter and brick mason. He used to tell me, that the best houses have smart blueprints. To make a great design, you must have smart worker to follow those blueprints for the best outcome. And the strongest part of the house is the foundation, so you start there first. I think, we must do the same thing with our lives.

142. God created the heaven and earth in six days. Who's to say He can't change your world in one day? - Unknown

God is a miracle worker, and He will never forsake you. Therefore, you could be God's next miracle at any moment.

143. Repentance is not when you cry to God. Repentance is when you change for God. - Unknown

Actions always speaks louder than words. Don't just talk about it. Be about it! Change is hard at times, but always worth it in the end.

144. Before God can greatly use you, He has to greatly hurt you first. - Unknown

Just like in the military boot camp, the main purpose is to break you down to recreate you as a stronger, wiser, focused, and better individual for the greater good of the team, mission, and purpose. God will do the same thing for His team, His mission, His purpose and His will.

145. **When you allow God to lead you through a trail, you get to see Him for yourself. - Dr. Tony Evans**

That's why we must have trials, suffering, and pain to be isolated and vulnerable enough to only need God during those hard times.

146. **Those who leave everything in God's hands will eventually see God's hands in everything. - Unknown**

And God's hands are better than All-State, Jerry Rice, Randy Moss, Willie Mays, and Kawhi Leonard are put together.

147. **Worrying is a conversation you have with yourself about things you cannot change. Prayer is a conversation with God about things He can change. - Unknown**

Have faith and trust God is hearing your prayers. Worrying is how you give the devil pleasure. So, focus on making God happy, so you can be happy.

148. **God always wants us to try our best. But when we can't, He just really wants us to trust and believe in Him. - Calvin Jackson**

God knows we are not perfect, but we should trust and believe Him perfectly. His will is the better than your plans. Always keep the faith during good and bad times.

Conclusion

God Said No!

I asked God to take away my habit. God said no. It is not for me to take away, but for you to give it up. I asked God to make my handicapped child whole. God said no. His spirit is whole & his body is temporary. I asked to grant me patience. God said no. Patience is a byproduct of tribulations; it isn't granted it is learned. I asked God to give me happiness. God said no. I give you blessings. Happiness is up to you. I asked God to spare my pain. God said no. Suffering draws you apart from worldly cares and brings you closer to me. I asked God to make my spirit grow. God said no. You must grow on your own, but I will prune you to make you fruitful. I asked God for all things that I might enjoy life. God said no. I will give you life, so that you may enjoy all things. I asked God to help me love others, as much as He loves me. God said Yes. You finally got the idea! - Unknown

May God bless you on your journey of life, during all your Moments of Truth. - Calvin Jackson

Part 2

Love & Happiness

1. **A person that over thinks, is also a person the over loves. -Unknown**

   As an over thinker, my mind runs non-stop. But so does my heart for the person I'm thinking about the most.

2. **Life is too short for fake love, fake connections, and fake relationships. - Calvin Jackson**

   Keep fake people away for your heart. Love can't be false on any level. We only have one life to live. Be happy and love truly.

3. **If you love life, life will love you back. - Unknown**

   Love your life and good things will happen within your life. Life is precious and should not be taken for granted.

4. **Follow your dreams, goals, passion, and calling in your life. Love your facts, not people's opinions. - Calvin Jackson**

   Make decisions for you and only you. People will put their insecurities on you, not because they don't love you, but because they don't understand you. Go for it!

5. **Love is a double-edged sword. A great weapon to have in life, but it sucks when you get cut and hurt from it. - Calvin Jackson**

   Be careful dealing with love. It can heal you or destroy you!

6. **Love your wife, kids, and family like God loves the church. - Unknown**

    To love how God loves means to love with no expectation, no judgement, no inconsistency, and to forgive with compassion with no evil in your heart.

7. **Don't force love, relationships, and friendships in life. Those things should be organic and should come to you naturally. - Calvin Jackson**

    When you have to force or beg for love from another person you disrespect yourself every time.

8. **You can't have love and trust without respect and loyalty. - Calvin Jackson**

    It's impossible! These strong traits go hand and hand. They need each other to survive in any relationship.

9. **Tell people you love them and give them their flowers while they are alive, not at a hospital on their death bed or funeral. - Calvin Jackson**

    Love is for the living to experience, share, and enjoy.

10. **If you love her mind, her body will follow. - Unknown**

    Women are mental and must have mental stimulation. So, kiss her mind and thoughts before her lips and body.

11. **Your heart knows things, your mind can't explain. - Unknown**

    The heart is full of feelings and the mind is logical. Sometimes love doesn't make sense, so your heart leads the way at times.

12. **Love is the only emotion that could involve every emotion. - Calvin Jackson**

    Love is the greatest emotion of all.

13. **Never give up on your spouse, kids, family, friends, and team. - Calvin Jackson**

    Quitting on people that care about you or that you care about is not a lovely situation.

14. **One of your life goals should be to love the person you see in the mirror as much as you can everyday. - Calvin Jackson**

    You must love yourself if you want to share and give love to others.

15. **Be careful who you love and trust. Sugar looks like salt and even the devil was an angel once.**

    Your love and trust is not for everybody. Some people don't deserve it. Use it wisely.

16. **True love has a habit of coming back around to you.- Calvin Jackson**

    You will never forget positive past relationships that changed your life for the better. Sometimes two people have to grow apart to grow as better people before they can grow together.

17. **Love what you do and do what you love. - Unknown**

    Love your job, career, major, dreams, plans, and goals. Also, love your coping skills, hobbies, and community as well.

18. **Love comes more naturally than hate to the human heart. - President Barack Obama**

    Love is already in our hearts from God, because God is love. Hate is something that is taught, learned, and developed over time by evil people.

19. **Being hated for being real is better than being loved for being fake.   - Calvin Jackson**

    Be true to yourself no matter what. That is a part of true happiness. If people don't like it, that's their problem.

20. **If you soak a person with love and praise the right way, they will drip of confidence and purpose. - Calvin Jackson**

    When you feed people love, great things start to happen in their life.

21. **Love people who love you, but never get attached to them. - Calvin Jackson**

    Things change and people change. Always remember, love can last forever, but nothing last forever.

22. **The hardest people to love are the ones that need love the most. - Unknown**

Everybody needs and wants love, but the people with pain and anger in their hearts need love more to counter act the negative thoughts before they become actions.

23. **Love is expressed in the vocabulary of action. - Mort Fertel**

We must not say we love and not show that same love in different acts of kindness. Remember, actions always speak louder than words.

24. **Happiness is life without expectations. - Elon Musk**

Do not put expectations on others. It only adds stress and pressure to the relationship or situation that is already difficult.

25. **Parents, always remember, tough love is still love. - Calvin Jackson**

Kids needs all types of love from parents to help them learn different lessons to prepare them for life. Therefore, as parents, we must not enable them by setting them up to fail.

26. **Don't let love blind you from your reality. - Calvin Jackson**

Love will have you dazed and unfocused at times. You will avoid red flags and other hazards that you would never overlook in your normal state of mind. Pay attention.

27. **Love and happiness come in all shapes, colors, styles, and sizes. Try them all! - Calvin Jackson**

    Don't put limits on love. Love is beautiful. Love is epic. Love is timeless. Love is everywhere.

28. **Happy people don't have to have the best of everything, because they just make the best out of everything. - Unknown**

    Happiness has nothing to do money and material things. It has everything to do with relationships with others and time spent with them to create the best memories.

29. **Happiness is an inside job. Don't give anyone that much power over your life. - Smillionaire**

    Happiness starts with you, nobody else. If you are happy, the people in your life you will be happy as well.

30. **Speak, act, move, think, dream, and pray like you love yourself - Calvin Jackson**

    Always take care of yourself. You are all you got.

Love Yourself First

In the dictionary, love means an intense feeling of deep affection and a great pleasure in something. Wikipedia defines love as a range of strong with positive emotional and mental states from the most sublime figure, good habit, to the deepest interpersonal affection to the simplest pleasure.

When I think of the word love, I just start to smile, because people and things you love make you happy and satisfied on every level. As a little boy, not really knowing what love was, I do remember saying God is love in my prayers and as my family blessed the food before we ate every mealtime. Therefore, to me, love is God-giving and something that everyone is born with. Love helps us feel emotions, think, and react. Love helps us understand self, family, and relationships as well.

We came into this world by ourselves, and we are leaving this world by ourselves. It only makes sense to love yourself to the fullest. It is vital to your success and mindset to have a blessed life. To move with love and compassion in your heart and to think with confidence and integrity are special traits few people have. Always be unselfish towards others and always have unconditional love for all your loved ones. But never forget to love yourself first.

We must always remember we are made in God's likeness and image. So, we must think highly and speak highly of ourselves, and then act accordingly. God wants us to love ourselves and show love to others everyday of our lives. Love is natural and organic, while hate is taught and convinced. Therefore, it is easier and makes more sense to love than hate.

We are all humans who have made bad mistakes and decisions in life. So, you will have bad days. But don't let bad days make you think you have a bad life. Don't let that negative energy stay within you too long either because you can block your blessing from God and from other people who are trying to help you. Remember, with God's love, you can improve any situation in your life.

One of the key components of loving yourself and finding true happiness is finding out what your personal, positive-coping skills are. Coping skills are the methods a person uses to deal with stressful situations. Basically, positive distractions that help you deal with hard times in life. Coping skills can be mental, spiritual, and physical. I love to teach positive coping skills at my job, because I know first-hand that they work. I notice that I feel better after I pray to God, help people, exercise, talk to my kids, hang out with my family and friends, reading knowledge, writing quotes, and preparing my podcast, "Numbers Don't Lie." Those are my coping skills.

Happiness is the main part of loving yourself. I'm blessed to able to do them all, too. Because I know life is too short to be unhappy. We must find things we love to do, by ourselves and with others. We must have goals and dreams in our minds and hearts too. Setting goals and achieving goals are all about self-love and self-esteem.

God put those thoughts in your mind for a reason. So, go for it and never quit!

No matter hard it is or how many times you fail. Get up and never give up! Use your energy, time, effort or love for your passion and purpose only. Don't use it on unworthy people, fake relationships, negative things, and hateful situations. Those things are what the devil, our enemy, sends to derail and distract you from your full potential and God's plan for you. Therefore, stay focused and love yourself first! Respectfully!

31. **Being happy and being loved are amazing blessings. Don't ever take them for granted. - Calvin Jackson**

    Love and happiness are the two greatest feelings in the world. They are true blessing from God.

32. **Love and marriage should be warm and welcoming like fresh cookies out the oven. Not cold and hard like the ice tray in the freezer. - Calvin Jackson**

    Real love is either hot or warm, but never cold.

33. **Love is a myth unless it comes from your mother, father, and kids. - Nas**

    Your mom, dad, kids, and grandparents are the foundations of love most of the time in your life. Take care of them.

34. **Marriage should be called or renamed to "The Ultimate Godly Love Friendship Teammate Challenge. " - Calvin Jackson**

    Because it's going to take to all those things to stay in love and stay together.

35. **Just don't be Eye Candy, love yourself enough to be a whole meal of Soul Food. - Calvin Jackson**

    Think about it. Eye Candy is temporary. Everybody remembers and loves Soul Food dinners at Big Mama's house.

36. **I love Netflix, but try to find someone you can build with, not just chill with. - Calvin Jackson**

    Relationships are more that kicking it and chilling. Build for the future if you really love the person you are with.

37. **Love is giving a person the power to destroy you and they don't. - Unknown**

    Unconditional love is also unconditional trust. Any relationship is nothing without love and trust. So, do the right thing by the people you love.

38. **If you married the wrong person, treat them like the right person and they will begin to act how you treat them. - Dr. Tony Evans**

    Marriage is what you make it. The love you show, with the work that you put into it, will tell what happens within it.

39. **Love what you have, before life teaches you to love what you lost. - Unknown**

    Don't ever take your loved one for granted. Things change and life can be crazy at times. You just never know what tomorrow holds.

40. **Happiness is the best emotion to experience, because all your other emotions help you realize how important happiness really is. - Calvin Jackson**

    Happiness is the release of stress, worry, depression, anxiety, and mood swings. It's one of the main keys of life. That's why we love it when we have it and must try to find it at all costs.

41. **Love is fading away when a spouse mumbles back, "I love you too," in an as low as a possible tone as their response to your "I love you." - Calvin Jackson**

    Pay attention to tone, cadence, pitch, and body language in your relationships. Communication is key and can happen in different ways.

42. **Deal with your problems, before your problems deal with your happiness. - Calvin Jackson**

    Stress will run your life if you let it. Find solutions to your problems and work on creating less turmoil in your life.

43. **Love will conquer all and will never fail, because God is love and He will never fail us. - Calvin Jackson**

    If you have God and love in your heart you will overcome all of your battles in life.

44. **Handling your business for money is a must, but handling your business with your loved ones is more important. - Calvin Jackson**

    Don't spend more time at work, at school, and staying busy, when you can spend time with your wife, kids, and family. Stay busy making memories with them, not being missed by them.

45. Know the difference between a Boo/Babe, Girlfriend/Boyfriend, Wifey/Hubby, Wife/Husband, & Soul Mate. - Calvin Jackson

There are levels to this. You can't show everyone the same love. You will get played! Some people don't deserve your love, time, and effort, because you can't get those things back.

46. Try to love, smile, and laugh even when you feel like you can't. -Calvin Jackson

Don't let your depression get the best of you. I know it's easier said than done, but that's a battle you must counteract to win.

47. Be easy to love, hard to break, and impossible to forget. - Calvin Jackson

Who wouldn't want a person with big heart full of love, mental toughness, and a legendary mind state?

48. Love is the person you think about during sad songs. - iLoveUofficial

Music reminds us of moments in time. Music inspires and is one of the best positive coping skills to use during negative times in your life.

49. Be happy in front of people who don't like you, it kills them. - Positive.thinking.zone

Misery loves company. So miserable people hate to see people happy! Be happy anyway!

50. **Loving a person that has never been loved properly will take a lot of patience. - Calvin Jackson**

    Love must be learned sometimes. People experience many things in life and some were never shown what real love is.

51. **Behind every "I Love You " lies a silent, "Please don't hurt me or break my heart. " - the.thoughts.power**

    It's hard to put yourself out there and love someone, especially when you don't know what the future holds, and things can change instantly.

52. **Put your ego on the shelf and love yourself. - Logic**

    You must put your ego and pride aside for the greater good. Having an ego is selfish, while loving others and loving yourself in not.

53. **Fake love is the worst kind of love. It's a real oxymoron! - Calvin Jackson**

    Fake anything is whack! It's not worth the time and effort to be fake or to entertain fake people. Be too real to be fake!

54. **If you want happiness and peace, you must prepare for war. - Unknown**

    Love, happiness, and peace are all hard to keep and maintain in a life. It can be hateful, cruel, and negative at times. But we must always fight for It!

55. **Love someone who is kinder to you than you are to yourself. - Calvin Jackson**

    The person you are with must love you, to understand your hardships to lift you up when you are down and out.

56. **Happiness is something you must create and design for yourself. Your happiness is not created and designed by another person. - Calvin Jackson**

    It's your life and you must be your own architect to happiness. Nothing will ever fall out the sky into your lap! Now, go get it!

57. **Your taste in people will change the more you love yourself. - Kev Crenshaw: The Heart Guy**

    The more you evolve and grow the better you become. So, loving yourself is making better decisions, spending time more wisely, and focusing on your goals. This might make some people disappear.

58. **Love: (noun) - Commitment to the well-being of others without conditions. - Webster's Dictionary**

    We need to know the definition of words to really understand how to use them.

59. **Don't make a person look stupid for loving you. - Unknown**

    Please don't disrespect your spouse, kids, and loved ones. Take care of your support system.

60. People glow differently when they are loved properly. - Unknown

We know people glow during their wedding, childbirth, graduation, baptism, etc. It's because their heart is full of joy, love, and happiness for their blessing

So, In Love…

The most memorable type of love is when you fall in love with someone else. Being in love with another person in your life is a special, rare and God-given gift. It is a perfect moment in time, when two people connect with happiness, energy, and vibes. The confidence and the butterflies in your stomach that love gives you creates a feeling of euphoria where you feel happiness, peace, and serenity in your heart, mind, and soul. Perfect harmony and true love between two people, with a major connection, is one of the greatest feelings in the world.

However, when love is lost from breakups or even worse circumstances, the feelings are the complete opposite. Heartbreak, anxiety, depression, over thinking and stress are a few symptoms caused from losing a loved one on any level. That's why it's crucial to love the right people and not waste time on the wrong people. You can't get time, effort, energy, or love back from people that don't feel the same way about you. However, we must remember, everything in life happens for a reason. So, we have to understand that with love it's either going to be a blessing or a lesson. We need both in life to grow and get better as people.

Love should not be forced, controlled, or confusing. Love should flow like the element of life down the Nile. Love should be a source from God to you and the person you're so in love with. Love should feel righteous, natural, peaceful, and sublime.

This is why love is the greatest emotion of all, because it has the power to affect all other emotions in your mind and body in a positive way or in a negative way.

Love has the power to make a person stay true and committed in a marriage to their high school sweetheart for 50 years or more. Love also has the power to make a person kill someone or themselves over a situation of love or heartbreak. Being in love is a blessing for sure, but it can be a burden at times as well.

Therefore, it is important to keep God involved in everything you do, and in all of your relationships in your life. God is love, so He will help and guide real relationships that have true love within them. And most importantly, God will restore you during sad and uncomfortable times too. Love is everlasting and unforgettable with the right person. Live in the moment with love, because you never know how long it's going to last? But love is so special, people say, "It's better to love and lose it, than to have never loved at all."

Some people don't ever experience real love in a genuine relationship with someone else during their lifetime. It's sad, but true. A loving relationship can be a little divine miracle with another person but it has to be perfectly timed by God. Love should never be rushed. We can't take being in love for granted either. We should do everything we can to keep real love alive in real relationships if they are worth it.

I do know that cheating, lying, and quitting has nothing to do with love in a real relationship.

Therefore, love the shit out of your significant other, wife, husband, spouse, partner, best friend, and soul mate with all your heart, mind, and soul. From the moment Cupid hits you in the butt with his love arrows, during the good and bad times, and even at the end of the relationship if things don't work out as planned.

Real love is also showing class, dignity, and respect to the other person at all times. I know it easier said than done, but at one time that person held a special place in your heart. Love hurts but love also heals. This journey called life is all about growth and getter better as a person. God's love, family love, being in love, showing love, sharing love, receiving love, and losing love are all experiences we need to help us reach our full potential of growth in our lifetime.

61. **Attraction is Flesh. Love is heart. Connection is soul. - Unknown**

    All three are awesome to have all at once!

62. **Love is a serious mental disease. - Plato**

    Love will bring out the craziness in people. Fighting, jealousy, envy, violence, abuse, suicide, etc. They can all be negative actions caused by heartbreak from love.

63. **You can't blame gravity for falling in love. - Albert Einstein**

    Love just happens sometimes, and there is nothing you can't do about it when it hits you. I got hit with Cupid's arrow when I didn't want to fall in love, but it wasn't up to me or her.

64. **Making love is composed of a single soul inhabiting two bodies. - Aristotle**

    Sex and making love are two different things. Both involve the body, but making love is done with the heart, mind, and soul.

65. **Nothing in the world smells as good as the person you love. - Staying_In_Love**

    The scent of your significant other should smell like heaven. Like fresh air to your nose and lungs.

66. **The key to happiness is doing things that feed the soul, not your ego. - bohemian. quotes**

    The ego kills all relationships. Happiness also comes from being humble.

67. **Intimacy and passion are not only about foreplay before sex. It's about the conversation, the eye contact, the touch, your tone, your laughter, your inspiration, your vibe, your energy, and your love before sex. - Calvin Jackson**

   "You're welcome." In My Kobe Bryant voice. LOL...

68. **Loving people is the smart and right thing to do. But never be dumb and wrong by doing so. - Calvin Jackson**

   People will take advantage of you and your love if you let them. Try to make intelligent love decisions about the people in your life.

69. **Don't worry. Be happy. - Bobby McFarland**

   You remember the 90's hit single with the catchy whistling sound. It's simple but true. Worrying leads to stress, anxiety, depression, and low self-esteem. So do your best to be and stay happy.

70. **The true way to real happiness is through the service of others. - David Meltzer**

   Love and happiness are not about money, materials, or status.

71. **Exercise is a great coping skill and resource for happiness. - Calvin Jackson**

   When your exercise your body releases endorphins to the brain than automatically improves your mood. Being fit and playing sports also builds confidence.

72. **Who we are and who we become depends, in part, on whom we love. - CoupleForward**

   Our loved ones will always affect our life. This is how an out-of-control man calms down to become a great father.

73. **People who love you don't love what you got and the people who love what you got don't love you. - Bishop TD Jakes**

   People are inconsistent; make sure the love you give and show is consistent.

74. **Love gives you hope; hope builds up faith; and faith brings you closer to God. - QuotesEmpire.com**

   God, love, hope, and faith will be needed to make it through this difficult life.

75. **Real love is not just based on romance, sex, dates, and fun times, it is mainly based on trust, loyalty, communication, and respect. - Calvin Jackson**

   All these things are important in a relationship. But it you want your relationship to last master the trust, loyalty, communication, and respect.

76. **Love and happiness are the only things that we can give without actually having. - Unknown**

   Happiness and love are the two gifts that keep on giving, and we should spread them as much as possible.

77. **Understanding your partner's traumas and triggers is another love language. - Unknown**

    You must know about your partner's trauma, so you can be understanding and positive for each other during hard those times.

78. **Joy is the sound of love, color of gratitude, and song of hope. - Coaching_By_Sharon**

    Don't ever let anyone steal your joy! It's yours for a reason, so find it at all costs.

79. **Unconditional love doesn't mean unconditional acceptance of bad behavior. - Kev Crenshaw**

    Just because you love someone, doesn't mean you can treat them any kind of way and accept anything they do. Kind behavior goes with unconditional love.

80. **Learn all the five love languages to help you love your partner better. - Calvin Jackson**

    Everybody is different; therefore, everybody gives and receives love differently. Give your relationship a real chance by knowing your partner's love language.

81. **Darkness cannot drive out darkness, only light can do that. Hate cannot drive out hate, only love can do that. - Dr. Martin Luther King, Jr.**

    Lead with your heart to love and make sure hate and evil stay away from your life.

82. **It's better to be hated for what you are than to be loved for what you are not. - Andre Gide**

    Always stay true to yourself by being yourself. Loving yourself is more important that others' opinions.

83. **Being deeply loved by someone gives you strength, while loving someone deeply gives you courage. - Lao Tzu**

    Love has the power to feed our soul, give us strength, helps our faith, and gives us courage to conquer fears in life.

84. **Tis better to have loved & lost, than never to have loved at all. - Lord Alfred Tennyson**

    If you have experienced real love, you are blessed. The experience and the lessons from love are priceless, even if you went through pain to learn them.

85. **Two people in love, alone, isolated from the world, that's beautiful. - Milan Kundera**

    Go on a date, take a hike, or a vacation with your partner. Just get away to come back better for each other.

86. **Be happy and thankful for what you have. Be fearless and relentless for what you want. - Soul_Chakras**

    Always be grateful and show gratitude in life. But if you want more and deserve better in your life, you got to go for it.

87. **Healing is an art. It takes time. It takes practice. It takes love. - The Seva Tree**

    Love cures all. And with time, help from loved ones, and you showing initiative for yourself, good things will start to happen. Healing can be difficult to paint at times, but make sure you evolve into a masterpiece over time.

88. **Real friends show their love in times of trouble, not in happiness. - Euripides**

    Having a great support system of family and friends could save your life one day.

89. **Love is the condition in which the happiness of another person is essential to your own. - Robert A. Heinlein**

    This is why love is unfair at times, because it's unpredictable! Some people will break your heart and others love your soul.

90. **My children have brought me so much happiness and joy. To me, they're the very true definition of Love. - Elizabeth Smart**

    Whenever I needed love, support, to smile, a hug, a positive conversation, and motivation I relied on my kids. They have no idea how they have saved my life and I need them more than they need me!

Parenthood
The Love that Lasts Forever

The greatest and largest responsibility God has blessed me with was being a father to my two beautiful, amazing children. My kids are my world! They are my main sources of focus and motivation. They have no idea how they saved my life. And I plan to show them every day that I'm forever grateful for them and their contributions that made me a better man on all levels. Without them, I would not know anything about patience, compassion, or forgiveness.

Only God can put your eyes, features, traits, and attributes in another person. To have a connection with another person that comes from your DNA and soul is the most epic connection and it lasts forever. It's truly a miracle and a blessing that some of us get to experience in a lifetime. Therefore, we should never stop thanking God for our kids and stay in a mindset to never take this blessing of parenthood for granted.

Another reason parenthood is a true blessing is because everyone could be parents, but not everyone should be parents. Very sad to say, but true. We all know what kind of horrible people exist in the world, and sometimes those people make horrible decisions from pain, heartbeat, poverty, abuse, environment, drug use, and any other negative situation that life might bring. It is everyone's responsibility to love, protect, and support kids at all costs. That's what God wants us to do as a village or community. Parenting is a tough, busy, unpredictable, demanding, and frustrating journey at times. Anything important you want to achieve in life is going to take hand work, planning, initiative, faith, love, and blessings from God to accomplish.

When I think about parenting, I think about the three types of love I saw from my parents and other great parents I know personally. Parenting is about tough love, realistic love, and unconditional love. Love is organic, natural, and from God. As parents, we must learn how to show these different types of love to be effective parents.

Parenting is about tough love sometimes. Real parents must make tough decisions for the greater good for their kids, because life is tough at times. There are times children must grow up fast, due to different situations and the family's dynamic. I know this all firsthand by being a hood kid of the 1990's in San Antonio, Texas.

I had poor friends and gangster family members, which made me see and understand that life is hard and unfair at times because of difficult situations. Tough love is setting those limits, rules, guidelines, morals, and values that will direct your children in the right way. No matter the situation, we must always do the right thing by teaching righteous qualities that build integrity and character. The two main traits needed for developing our children's character are critical thinking and positive decision making. These will carry them when you are no long around to help them. Just make sure you don't push your children away by being too tough on them. Tough Love is supposed to teach your children lessons, not breakdown them down and cause distance to grow between you.

Parenting is about realistic love as well. We must support and love our children at all costs. We must understand

and realize your kid's life is not your life. It's their life and their life only. Therefore, let them find it and live it. Like it or not, it their journey. You're just there to help, guide, and provide. So, don't live your dreams through your children's dreams.

Your job as a great parent is to help them create and achieve their own dreams. God gives everybody their own dreams, goals, and purpose to achieve in life. Your support in your kids dreams will show them the type of love that they will remember forever. And most importantly, they will know how to support and help their children in the future because of you.

Always keep it real with you kids, too. This is how a strong line of communication is built. Being real and honest creates ways to have tough conversations that must be had between a child and parent. And tough conversations lead to tough bonds that will never broken. All types of love have to be real to last forever.

Lastly, parenting needs unconditional love. This type of love is the most important to me for many reasons. It's all about compassion, understanding, support, communication, and forgiveness. This is the type of love that parents should show during bad times and disappointments. This is the love God gives us. It only makes sense to give this love to our children, family, and loved ones. However, unconditional love is the hardest love to give and show because the heart and the mind can only take so much heartbreak and disappointment. That's why it's so vital for great parents to have a short-term memory. That way everybody involved can move on and learn how to be better in and through the situation. Bad parents have a short fuse and are quick to explode which leads to frustration, arguments, poor communication, and the negative emotions children hold on to in their minds and hearts. The best parents show the attributes of Jesus to really make a difference in their children's lives.

God wants us to build quality relationships with our children and grandchildren. We must remember all meaningful relationships take a vast amount of hand work, focus, patience, trust, communication, and dedication. So never give up or quit on your kids. They will need your love, advice, help, and prayers with so many situations during their journey of life. These are things kids need daily. Therefore, it is a must to pray for them daily too. God answers prayers and will provide safety, love, welfare, support, and security for your children. Remember life is hard, so be a blessing to your children to help them during the hard times.

91. **Happiness is not a luxury. It's a necessity. When we are happy we are in the best possible place to be good to ourselves and to those we love. - Suze Roman**

    We must find love and happiness to take care of ourselves, which will help lead us in taking care of others properly.

92. **I believe in true love, and I believe in happy endings. ... And I believe! - Christine Brinkley**

    You must believe it to achieve it! No matter how bad life gets always believe in a brighter day to improve your life.

93. **Love is pure and true. Love knows no gender. - Tori Spelling**

    Love knows no color, race, sex, or status. Love is for everybody to experience during their life. Once again, God is Love.

94. **Immature love says... I love you because I need you. Mature love says... I need you because I love you. - Erich Fromm**

    Being immature versus mature is a big difference when communicating within a relationship.

95. **Love is when you sing to your partner out loud in public, even if you can sing or not. - Calvin Jackson**

    Showing love publicly is another way to validate and represent how much you love your relationship.

96. **The biggest coward of a man is to awaken the love of a woman without the intention of loving her. - Bob Marley**

Don't play games with the mind or the heart. Sometimes those organs are very fragile. Be mature enough to be honest with yourself and others.

97. **A simple "I love you" means more than money. - Frank Sinatra**

Love is more valuable than money, and it lasts longer too.

98. **You don't marry someone you can live with. You marry someone you cannot live without. - Unknown**

Your soulmate is the person you need near your mind, body, heart, and soul to help you through life.

99. **Love is something sent from heaven to worry the hell out of you. - Unknown**

Nobody ever said love was easy and it can be stressful at times. Things we love will always concern us.

100. **Get someone willing to start fresh with you, struggle with you, grind with you, to build with you. - Calvin Jackson**

Building a life with someone you love in a true blessing. It's how couples grow together as one.

101. Happiness is when what you think, what you say, and what you do are in harmony. - Mahatma Gandhi

Gandhi was very loving, wise, and spiritual. Thinking, speaking, and doing are three blessings we should never take for granted.

102. Love and happiness are complementary. You cannot have one without the other, and you get the best of them together. - TheRightMessage.com

It's simple. Some things go perfect together. Peanut butter and jelly, cookies & milk, bacon and eggs, ebony and ivory, Kool-Aid and sugar, fish and chips, steak and potatoes, etc. But love and happiness is the ultimate combo on this list!

103. Two things prevent us from happiness: Living in the past and observing others. - @ LifeHack

It is very unhealthy to think about things you can't change or control. What's meant for you will be yours. So, don't compare your life to others. Live for the present and the future, because you can control that.

104. Always find time for things that make you feel happy to be alive. - Unknown

In a life that can be led by trials and tribulations, it is a must for you to learn and experience positive coping skills to make you happy in order to counteract the negative events in your life.

105. **The only thing that will make you happy is being happy with who you are and not who people think you are. - Goldie Hawn**

Never please people with false pretenses. Being yourself is the way to please yourself, and the right people will gravitate to you.

106. **Fall in love with those who let your heart beat at its own pace. - Matt Tarragon**

Love cannot be rushed or timed; it just happens. And everybody gives and receives love differently; so be patient with your partner.

107. **The Bible does not say, "Money is the root of all evil. " It says, "The Love of money is..." We are called to manage money for God not to worship it. - Dave Ramsey**

We should only worship and love God. Money is a big part of life, but don't let it control your life. Managing, saving, earning, investing, giving, and helping others with money are blessings from God as well.

108. **To be brave is to love someone unconditionally without expecting anything in return. – Madonna**

Loving someone is always a huge risk. But no matter what happens, set expectation only for yourself.

109. **I Love you like a fat kid loves cake. - Biggie**

Now that's real love! Find the simple joy, mental pleasure, and inner happiness with the one you love.

110. Never let your new love pay for the troubles that your ex-love put you through. - HeartbreakQuote

Do not let past failed relationships dictate your current or future ones. Be progressive in your relationships. Remember, the "L" stands for lessons, not losses.

111. At the touch of love, everyone becomes a poet. - Plato

Love puts your heart and mind at ease and brings peace and serenity to your soul, just like poetry.

112. My love for you is past the mind, beyond the heart, and into my soul. - Boris Kodjoe

Love will affect your mind, body, and soul and will grow each day when the person is worth it.

113. I have decided to stick to love. Hate is too great of a burden to bear. - Dr. Martin Luther King, Jr.

It's always easier to love, than to get envy in your heart and hate. For example, it takes less face muscles to smile, than it does to frown. Love is light. Hate is heavy.

114. For "Love Gumbo" you're going to need God, love, loyalty, respect, communication, comprehension, intimacy, passion, initiative, and forgiveness. -Bon appetite.

Everyone makes their gumbo uniquely, with different ingredients. Just make sure you just add in only the good ones.

115. **Folks are usually about as happy as they make their minds up to be. - Abraham Lincoln**

Your mind will dictate how you feel, how you act, and how you express yourself. It always starts with you!

116. **Happiness comes in waves. It will find you again. - Unknown**

Storms happen during bad seasons in our life but they are temporary. So, don't lose hope or faith during dark times. You will appreciate the sunshine more when it comes back.

117. **Happiness is letting go of what you think your life is supposed to look like. - Unknown**

Stop setting expectations on your timing and never set expectations from other people. Timing is up to God and other people will change on you. Just let go and go with the flow.

118. **If you want happiness for an hour, take a nap. If you want happiness for a day, go fishing. If you want happiness for a year, inherit a fortune. If you want happiness for a lifetime, help someone else. - Chinese Proverb**

Resting, relaxing, getting money, and being a blessing to others is a great life to live.

119. **When one door of happiness closes, another opens. But often we look so long at the closed door that we do not see what has been opened for us. - Helen Keller**

    Don't miss your blessing because you are stressing over your burden.

120. **Happiness is a state of activity. - Aristotle**

    When depressed, you must stay positive, busy, productive, determined, focused, and disciplined, so you don't have time to feel sad. Love yourself enough to fight off sadness and depression.

Loving & Helping Others

The main thing about love is that it can last forever, and it's just as good to give love as it is to receive love. Showing love, feeling love, and giving love to yourself and others are major part of life. Life is better when love is within you. It helps us to cope during hard times and appreciate the good times. Love is everlasting, because God is love. Therefore, we must love, give, share, care, and talk to our loved ones, friends, associates, and strangers during our journey of life. Yes, that right, strangers too.

Loving family and friends can be very difficult at times, but still easier than loving complete strangers whom you just met or someone you don't know. God doesn't want us to show love only when it's easy or convenient for us. Love should flow from everywhere and should never stop. God wants us to give and receive love in every way possible so we can experience Him in every way possible, especially during this time and era of Co-Vid 19, the war between Russia and Ukraine, homelessness, racism, gender equality, abortion rights, crimes, violence, and so many types of mental illness.

Love is a feeling that must be shared and experienced, not just talked about. But more importantly, love is an action that can be used every day to help change the world. And we should want to be the change we want to see in the world.

As a student, teacher, coach, and recreation activity specialist, I always want to learn new things from successful, self-aware, motivated, and knowledgeable people.

So, I have read books and quotes by Eric "E.T." Thomas, Les Brown, Zig Ziglar, Tony Robbins, David Meltzer, Dave Ramsey, Steven Furtick, Michael Todd, Dr. Tony Evans, T.D. Jakes, Max Lucado to name a few Yoda's of mine. All these gentlemen help people all over the world to become better people in many areas of their lives.

All of them have stated in way that the true source, action, and mind state to love and happiness are done by giving back in some way to help other people in need. Basically, showing love to others will automatically improve your attitude, mind, and heart during anytime in your life which will lead to better gratitude, karma and energy in our lives as well. This makes total sense because God rewards the golden hearted.

When I put a smile on someone else face it always makes me smile. Helping others and paying it forward are great ways to show love. They are major parts of life because we all need help at some time in our lives. Life is full of ups and downs with many good and bad times. Therefore, your act of kindness could make a positive difference that could change everything in that person's life. And you could even save a life in doing so.

The Bible tells us in many scriptures that we should help the poor, sick, homeless, orphans, widows, and the heartbroken. Love yourself always, but always show love others too. You must show love and bless others if you want love and blessings from God and the universe.

Try to find a way to show love to others in need and help a negative situation become more positive. It can be simple, easy, and cheap too. It will make the world a better place and make you a better person in the process. You can find a church, program, or organization that needs your help, or you can create a way to give back in your own way. For example, my mom (who is a great mother, grandmother, and great grandmother by the way) buys diapers and wipes for newborns for families in need.

When she told me about it, I was amazed that a woman in her 70's was showing such initiative to help others. It has compelled me to show more initiative, effort, and compassion to help others now. I asked my mom why she started doing that? She replied, "No mother should worry about keeping their baby clean. Being a parent is hard enough and any type of help is a blessing." Lastly, she said, "And Calvin, I just love babies! They are so beautiful and precious. They are God's little angles on earth and we have to love them so they will know what love feels like and continue to be with God." Wow, I immediately started to think about what more I could do. Donating old clothes wasn't enough anymore for me. I needed to start my own way to give back and start a cool way to do so, like my mom had done.

I started thinking and praying about it, and a few days later I created the Blessing Box, a middle-sized box in my back seat floor filled with water, snacks, chips, small Bibles, hand sanitizer, t-shirts, hand towels, masks, napkins, and one dollar bills to help homeless people while

I drive to random places around the city. I don't have a lot of money, so most of the stuff comes from the H.E.B., Wal-Mart, and the Dollar Store. But I knew I had to do more to show love to strangers and help others in need.

I know my effort is like putting a band-aid on a laceration, but I'm not going to just talk about it anymore. I want to play and coach in the game of life and make a difference. No matter how big or small. I do know it takes a village to help the community, so this is me doing my part. I challenge you to find or create a lane, organization, or situation you can make a positive difference in. The world has many problems, so there is always something that needs our help and positive solutions. We need more positive actions, uncomfortable conversations, faith, love, and being consistent when facing problems. However, it is done, it's up to us to try to change those problems into victories and testimonies.

I'm a firm believer in, "teamwork makes the dream work." And with God on your side you can achieve anything in the world. God will continue to show and prove that nothing is impossible with him. Due to that fact, God will always give love, grace, and mercy to the people who support His plan and will.

121. I'd far rather be happy than right any day. - Douglas Adams

Remember this during times of stress or arguing with your partner...Who cares who's right? It's about understanding and moving on at the end of the day. I was a dumb, factual husband who always wanted to be right. I wasted a lot of time being selfish and having pride. Meanwhile, both of us were still unhappy, mad, and sad afterwards. Focus on happiness and forgiveness.

122. Just because your love didn't last forever, doesn't mean it wasn't worth your while. - Unknown

Real family and friendship last forever. And if kids are involved, it was really worth it. Learning from everything to better yourself is a plus, too. An old true saying goes.... "It's better to love and to have lost, than not to have been loved at all."

123. Learn to let go. That is the key to happiness. - Buddha

This was the hardest thing for me to do, but it must be done to completely heal your pain and heartbreak. I know it's easier said than done, but you must let go and let God in order for you to grow.

124. Optimism is a happiness magnet. If you stay positive, good things and good people will be drawn to you. - Mary Lou Retton

It's important to always put positive vibes and energy in the universe. You will get it back and others will want to start being a positive person like you.

125. **Be loving. Be focused. Be smart. Be crazy. Be weird. Be silly. Be whatever. Because life is too short to be anything but happy. - Unknown**

Always be your true self. Always respect and love yourself. Always live life to the fullest and dream big. And always focus on your happiness and go for it. Because life it not meant for anything else.

126. **Just don't show love and appreciation to your friends and family on Thanksgiving and Christmas. Every day is a holiday. - Calvin Jackson**

Love should be shown all year round, not when the world tells you to show love.

127. **There will be a time when strangers and associates will show you more love, than friends and family. - Calvin Jackson**

Love is love. Take it and appreciate it. It's better than no one loving you at all. Sometimes your people will take you for granted.

128. **Everyone you meet will come with baggage. Find someone who loves you enough to never give up on you and someone who helps you unpack. - Unknown**

Nobody is perfect and we all have flaws. So, help your loved one grow and evolve to the next level by loving them and believing in them.

129. **Happiness is the secret to all beauty. There is no beauty without happiness. - Christian Dior**

    Try to find happiness and beauty in everything. Because, without it, things in life are dark, bland, and mediocre.

130. **The best proof of love is trust, respect, and loyalty. – Dr. Joyce Brothers**

    True story! Agreed!

131. **The six-word love story: I can't imagine life without you. -Anonymous**

    It's a great love story and a great feeling if your significant other tells you this. But if you feel this way and they don't feel the same, it can turn into a horror story real quick.

132. **The way to love anything is to realize that it may be lost. - Gilbert K. Chesterton**

    Nothing in life lasts forever, so be ready for anything. But it's important to show the one you love that you are going to love them now, not later.

133. **Love grows by giving. The love we give away is the only love we keep. - Elbert Hubbard**

    True happiness comes from the service and the love we show others. Being kind can go a long way.

134. **Love does not consist of gazing at each other but looking outward together in the same direction. - Antonie de Saint-Exupery**

    Having dreams, setting goals, and building a foundation for your family is going to take great planning, strong communication, and being on the same page to grow.

135. **A person does not know what real love is until, they have lost it and never found it again. - Calvin Jackson**

    You never know what you got until it's gone. Take care of your loved one and take nothing for granted. Love is precious for a reason.

136. **Being deeply loved by someone gives you strength, while loving someone deeply gives you courage. - Lao Tzu**

    Love can achieve and conquer all! But it must be true, real, and unconditional.

137. **Other people loving you is a bonus. You loving yourself is the real prize. - Unknown**

    Self-love is the best love. All you have is yourself! You must love yourself to really love other people in life.

138. **Someone who loves you wouldn't put themselves in a position to lose you. - Trent Shelton**

    True love is about showing compassion, effort, and care. If the other person is not showing initiative like you are, communicate and find out why.

139. **Never apologize for being deeply in love with a person. - Calvin Jackson**

The heart wants what the heart wants. If it works out or not, love is always special. However, always control your emotions dealing with love.

140. **You know it's love when all you want is that person to be happy, even if you're not part of their happiness. - Julia Roberts**

Letting go of the person you love is always hard, but if they don't love you anymore, why hold on? Showing unselfishness, respect, and class by wishing them well is an act of real love.

141. **Knowing your goals and purpose keeps you loving, focused and happy in life. - Calvin Jackson**

Positive thoughts and positive actions will lead to positive situations in life.

142. **Don't chase love, let love chase you. - Unknown**

It's really simple. Don't chase. Get chosen! What's meant to be will be.

143. **Real love should be organic and natural. So, fall in love without even knowing when, where, and how. - Calvin Jackson**

Love is a great force of nature. Therefore, it will find you because we are a part of the same great force of nature.

144. **Love is all about handling hard times with care and compassion. - Calvin Jackson**

     If you really love your kids, wife, family, and friends show them love, patience, understanding, and love when they mess up or need your help during a difficult time.

145. **When you like a flower, you pluck it. When you love a flower, you will water it daily. - Buddha**

     This goes for anything you love in life. Significant others, family, friends, kids, education, career, and yourself will need to be watered to keep growing and evolving.

146. **When you move with love and your intentions are pure, you don't lose anyone, they lose you. - Nipsey Hussle**

     If you loved then unconditionally, treated them like family, and were loyal to them, and they still did you wrong, it their loss not yours.

147. **Men need to be loved physically in order to love emotionally. Women need to be loved emotionally in order to love physically. - Unknown**

     Men and women are different on many levels, but both are equally important for a successful relationship.

148. Love in its essence is a spiritual fire. - Senenca

Therefore, two people in love must work hard to keep it lit. From putting more "love wood chips" on it, blowing sweet kisses on it for more wind, and protecting it from rainstorms will keep it going towards forgiveness and compassion.

149. The greatest two healing therapies are true friendships and true love. - Hubert H. Humphrey

Agreed. My friends are really like my brothers, who continue to help and guide me through tough times. And God is love. We will always need love in our lives to make it better.

150. A successful marriage requires falling in love many times at different times, and always with the same person. - Mignon McLaughlin

Marriage is a very difficult relationship to maintain and evolve through the years. Since there are going to be many ups and downs, it's important to never quit on each other so the relationship can experience love through the test of time. And without testing, we don't have testimonies to help yourself and others.

Conclusion

You Make Me

You make me laugh when I want to cry,
Make me live when I want to die.
Make me smile when I want to frown,
You turn my life upside down.
Believe in me when no one else does.
You're my now, my is, and my was.
I'm afraid people notice I need you so much.
When I'm with you time flies by fast.
It's like the present is the past.
I need you more than you can believe.
Love you more than you can conceive.
Think about you every night and day,
And hope my life can stay this way.
I don't want it to be any other way.
- Unknown

CPSIA information can be obtained
at www.ICGtesting.com
Printed in the USA
LVHW021511191122
733280LV00027B/2012